Contents

About this book with
Foreword by Archbishop Vincent Nichols

Walking on water — 6
On the possibility of holiness

Prudence — 10
On choosing God's will (with St Gianna Molla)

Justice — 16
On fighting for what is right (with St David Roldán-Lara)

Fortitude — 22
On living a life of forgiveness (with St Josephine Bakhita)

Temperance — 28
On putting aside the things of this world (with Bl Pier Giorgio Frassati)

Virtuous living — 34
On the cardinal virtues and our own path to God

Daily Prayers — 39
Prayers from Sunday to Saturday

Supplementary resources including — 54
Quotes on holiness and sanctity, a thought for the day & films to watch

Sparks of Light

Sparks of Light
978-0-9570793-2-8

Nihil Obstat: Father Anton Cowan, Censor
Imprimatur: The Most Reverend Vincent Nichols, Archbishop of Westminster
Date: Ash Wednesday 22 February 2012

The Nihil obstat *and* Imprimatur *are a declaration that a book or pamphlet is considered to be free from doctrinal or moral error. It is not implied that those who have granted the* Nihil obstat *and* Imprimatur *agree with the contents, opinions or statements expressed.*

Writing Group: Dr Mark Nash, Fr Michael O'Boy, Ms Clare Ward, Mrs Margaret Wickware

The Diocese of Westminster's Agency for Evangelisation is grateful to the National Council of the Churches of Christ in the U.S.A for use of the New Revised Standard Version Bible: Catholic Edition copyright © 1993 and 1989. Excerpts from The Divine Office © 1974, hierarchies of Australia, England and Wales, Ireland. All rights reserved.

All of the images contained in this booklet have been taken from those freely available at the Wikimedia Commons website.

Produced by Agency for Evangelisation, Vaughan House, 46 Francis Street, London, SW1P 1QN. Tel: 020 7798 9152; email: evangelisation@rcdow.org.uk

In collaboration with the Home Mission Desk of the Catholic Bishops' Conference of England and Wales http://www.catholic-ew.org.uk/

 booklets are published by WRCDT. Design by Mark Nash.
Print arranged by Transform Management Ltd
info@1025transform.co.uk

Copyright © 2012, Diocese of Westminster, Archbishop's House, Ambrosden Avenue, London, SW1P 1QJ. All rights reserved.

 The Diocese of Westminster's Agency for Evangelisation is committed to a sustainable future for our planet. The booklet in your hands is made from paper certified by the Forest Stewardship Council.

Foreword

Dear Brothers and Sisters,

In this faith-sharing resource the lives of four modern saints will be set before us. Each had choices to make - choices that involved suffering, pain and even death - but each held to what they believed to be right and true. It is tempting to focus on the extraordinary acts of these saints but such heroism, as you will see, was the fruit of ordinary lives, well lived; lives where the virtues of faith, hope and charity were cultivated in prayer and sacrament.

Announcing the Year of Faith (11 October 2012 – 24 November 2013) in which he notes the fiftieth anniversary of the Second Vatican Council and the twentieth anniversary of the new Catechism, Pope Benedict reminds us that our witness - the way in which we live our lives in the world - is central to the Church's renewal. 'Christians', he says 'are called to radiate the word of truth that the Lord Jesus has left us'.

This resource takes its name from some words of Blessed Pope John XXIII, who convened the Second Vatican Council:

'Every believer in this world must be a spark of light, a core of love, life-giving leaven in the mass: and the more he is so, the more he will live, in his innermost depths, in communion with God.'

My desire is that this faith-sharing resource will help you see that 'saintly' living is as much for you as it has been for anyone, and that you will explore how in the seeming ordinariness of daily living you can be an effective agent, a spark of light, in the Church's mission today.

Yours devotedly,

+ Vincent Nichols

The Most Reverend Vincent Nichols
Archbishop of Westminster

About this book

'It is not easy for man, wounded by sin, to maintain moral balance. Christ's gift of salvation offers us the grace necessary to persevere in the pursuit of the virtues. Everyone should always ask for this grace of light and strength, frequent the sacraments, cooperate with the Holy Spirit, and follow the Spirit's calls to love what is good and shun evil' (Catechism of the Catholic Church, 1811).

The *Catechism of the Catholic Church* lists seven virtues which are broken into two parts: the human virtues (prudence, justice, fortitude and temperance) and the theological virtues (faith, hope and love). It is the practice of these, with the gift of God's grace, that brings us to sanctity.

Sparks of Light is divided into six group sessions. Sessions One and Six look at holiness in general terms while sessions Two, Three, Four and Five look at the human virtues through the lives of four saints who lived and died within living memory. As mentioned in the foreword, the title of this resource has been taken from the words of Blessed Pope John XXIII.

In addition to the Scripture and reflections now familiar to users of *exploring faith* booklets, you will find a short biography of the relevant saint - reading this will give you a clearer understanding of their lives though can be omitted during the session if time is short. The Scripture passages have been chosen to reflect the theme of their respective sessions but you will benefit from reading the passage in context (that is, reading the passages before and after the one chosen) either as a group or individually.

The group sessions are illustrated with a selection of pictures arranged in a semblance of what the Eastern Churches call an iconostasis - looking upon these images of the saints may stir a thought or feeling in a way that the text could not. We also invite you to make use of the daily prayers in the second part of the booklet which are drawn from the Divine Office.

Sparks of Light is not tied to a particular time of year and the prayers and meditations may be used by individuals, groups or in a wider parish context throughout the year. Additional reflections and thoughts can be found on our small group blog - *a threefold cord is not easily broken* [http://dowsmallgroups.wordpress.com]. This booklet and others in the *exploring faith* series can be viewed at and downloaded from http://issuu.com/exploringfaith/docs/.

'ICONOSTASIS' APOSTLES

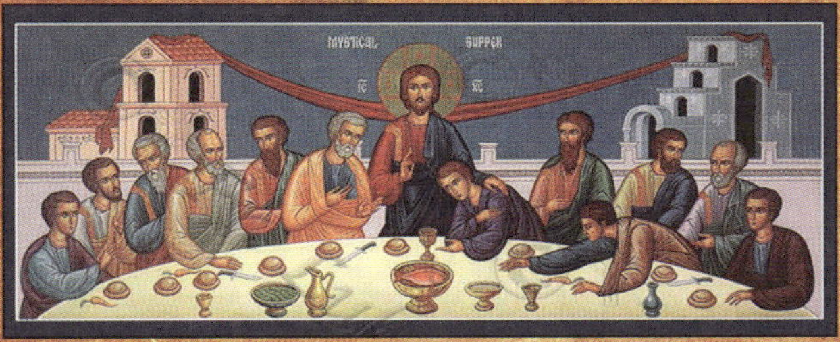

16

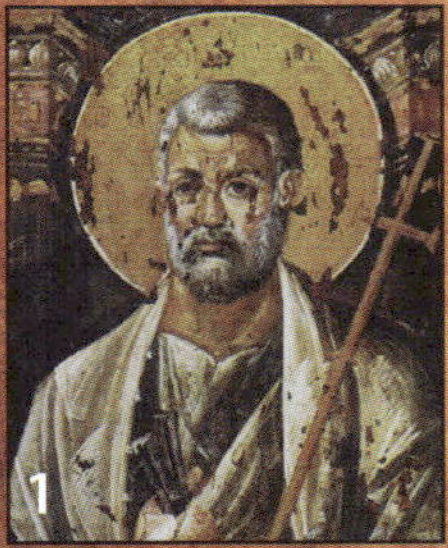
1

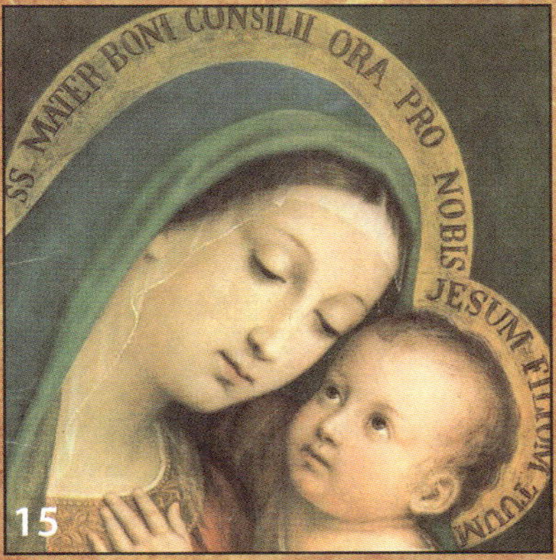

15

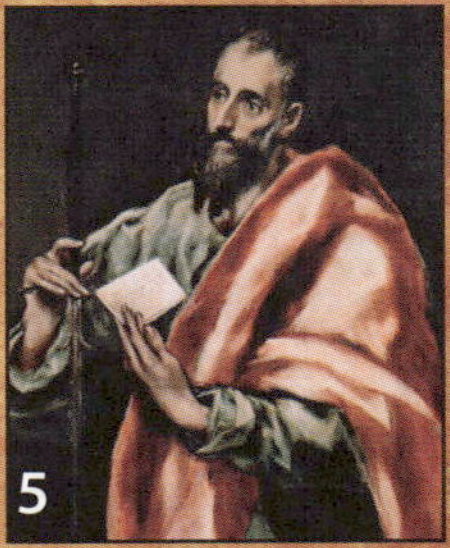
5

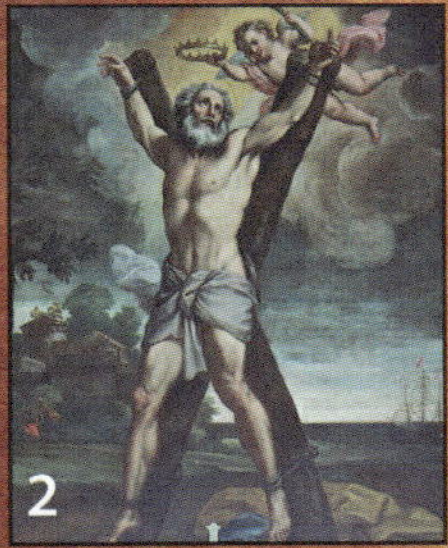
2

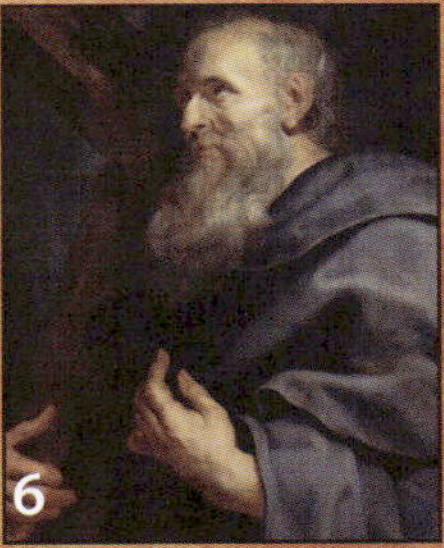
6

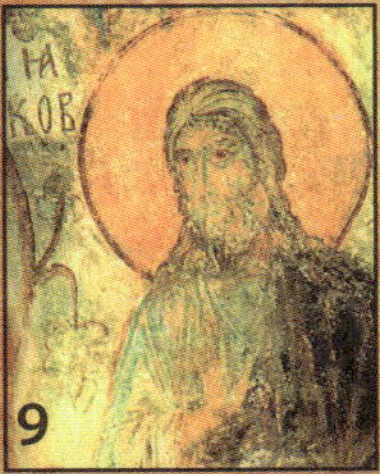
9

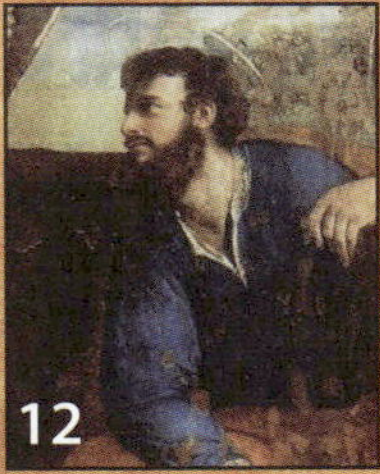
12

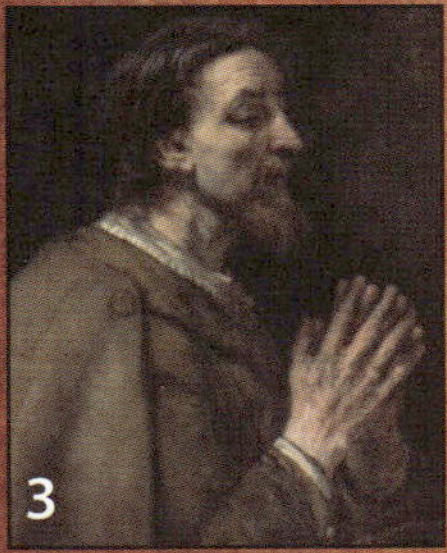
3

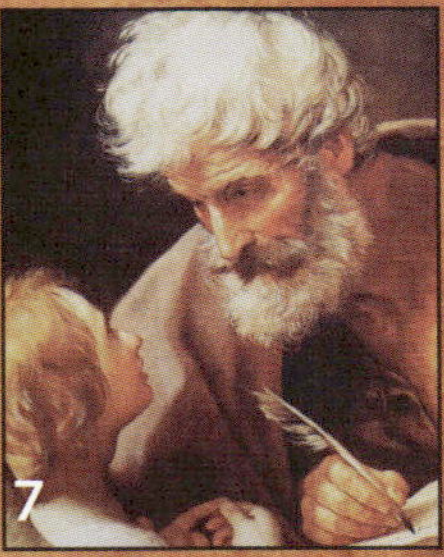
7

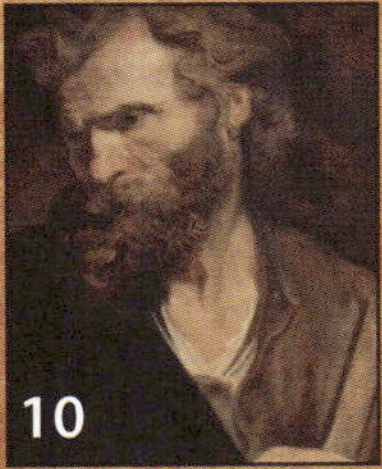
10

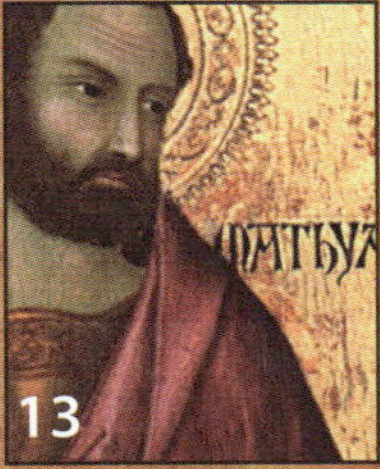
13

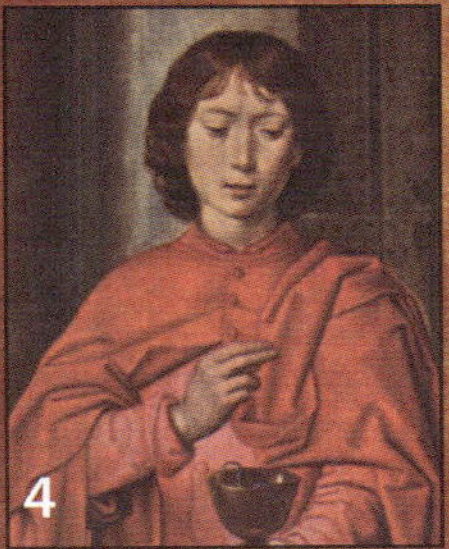
4

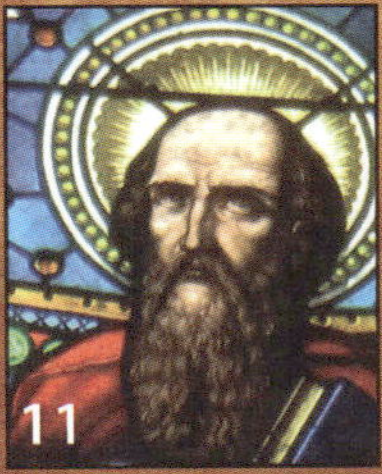
11

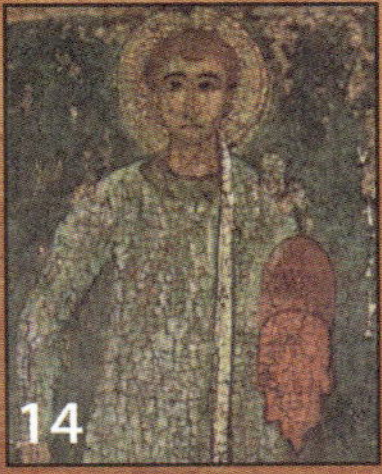
14

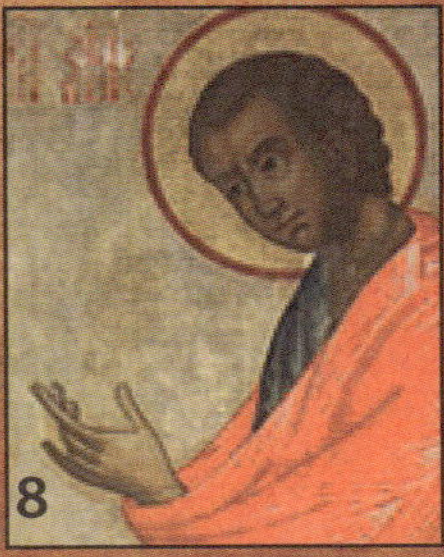
8

. St Peter (died c.AD64); 2. St Andrew; 3. St James the Greater (44); 4. St John; 5. St Paul (c.67); 6. St Philip (c.80); 7. St Matthew c.60); 8. St Thomas (c.72); 9. St James the Lesser; 10. St Thaddeus; 11. St Simon (c.65 or 107); 12. St Bartholemew; 13. St Matthias c.80); 14. St Stephen (c.34); 15: Our Lady of Good Counsel and the Christ Child; 16. The Last Supper

Walking on water

Opening Prayers
Taken from Psalm 8

All: How great is your name, O Lord our God,
through all the earth!

Leader: Your majesty is praised above the heavens;
on the lips of children and of babes
you have found praise to foil your enemy,
to silence the foe and the rebel.

Group: When I see the heavens, the work of your hands,
the moon and the stars which you arranged,
what are we that you should keep us in mind,
men and women that you care for us?

Leader: Yet you have made us little less than gods;
and crowned us with glory and honour,
gave us power over the works of your hands,
put all things under our feet.

All: How great is your name, O Lord our God,
through all the earth!

All: Glory be to the Father, and to the Son and to the Holy Spirit. As it was in the beginning, is now, and ever shall be, world without end. Amen.

As we come together let us, either aloud or in the silence of our hearts, give thanks and praise to the Lord for all the things we have accomplished, the joys experienced, graces received and people met over the past week. Let us also remember all those in need of our prayers.

Introduction to the Scripture reading
Let us listen carefully to the Word of the Lord,
and attend to it with the ear of our hearts.
Let us welcome it, and faithfully put it into practice.

St. Benedict of Nursia (c.480-c.547) adapted

Sparks of Light

session one

Explore the Scriptures Matthew 14:22-33
Immediately he made the disciples get into the boat and go on ahead to the other side, while he dismissed the crowds. And after he had dismissed the crowds, he went up the mountain by himself to pray. When evening came, he was there alone, but by this time the boat, battered by the waves, was far from the land, for the wind was against them. And early in the morning he came walking towards them on the lake. But when the disciples saw him walking on the lake, they were terrified, saying, 'It is a ghost!' And they cried out in fear. But immediately Jesus spoke to them and said, 'Take heart, it is I; do not be afraid.'

Peter answered him, 'Lord, if it is you, command me to come to you on the water.' He said, 'Come.' So Peter got out of the boat, started walking on the water, and came towards Jesus. But when he noticed the strong wind, he became frightened, and beginning to sink, he cried out, 'Lord, save me!' Jesus immediately reached out his hand and caught him, saying to him, 'You of little faith, why did you doubt?' When they got into the boat, the wind ceased. And those in the boat worshipped him, saying, 'Truly you are the Son of God.'

Please take a few moments in silence to reflect on the passage, then share a word or phrase that has struck you. Pause to think about what others have said then, after a second reading of the passage, you may wish to share a further thought.

Reflection

I never imagined I would fly, but I did. I never believed that I could write, but I can. I never thought I would be able to live through this time of grief, but I have? Life is full of challenges we feel we are not up to, but somehow, somewhere along the way, bridges are crossed and what once seemed beyond us, is suddenly behind us – and not, necessarily, because there was any great plan, more that it was a matter of getting through, coping and moving on.

I doubt that Peter ever contemplated walking on water but, as we are told in the gospel, he did exactly that. The Lord has not called us to walk on water, but he has called us to holiness and this, like so many other things, can seem a challenge too far. Asked what holiness looks like, most of us would draw on the example of others – some famous, some not so famous – few would point to themselves. Holiness is for others, not for me. But if we take time to stand back and reflect on our own lives and the lives of those closest to us – those whose faults we know – we will discover holiness: the holiness of parents making sacrifices for their

Sparks of Light

children, the holiness of a neighbour's generosity, the holiness found in people's commitment to the Eucharist and to prayer

Christ did not call Peter to the impossible. It was Peter's lack of faith, not the impossibility of the task, that led him to sink. In baptism we were permanently marked by the gift of God's Holy Spirit. More particularly, we did not receive a sample, a share or a taste of the Spirit. No, we received the Spirit in all its power and glory – the same Spirit that hovered over the waters and brought the world to life, the same Spirit that rose Jesus from the dead, the same Spirit who empowered the Apostles at Pentecost, banishing their fear and filling them with confidence. Holiness is not something out there beyond our reach, rather it is the exploration and unleashing of the gift – already given - that dwells within. What sense can there be in making excuses, what possible objection could there be, when the invitation to holiness is the invitation to explore what you have and to be what you are…truly, simply, radically…the image of God. God, who has shared in our humanity so that each of us, through the action of the Holy Spirit, may share in his divinity. 'Lord, if it is you, command me to come to you on the water', and the Lord says, 'Come'.

What part does silence play in my prayer? Where do I take the time to listen to what Christ might be saying to me? Where, in the business of daily living, could I find space for silence?

Sparks of Light

Closing Prayers
You may wish to end this session with some different prayers, the Our Father or silent reflection.

As we adore you, O God, who alone are holy
and wonderful in all your Saints,
we implore your grace,
so that, coming to perfect holiness in the
    fullness of your love,
we may pass from this pilgrim table
to the banquet of our heavenly homeland.
Through Christ our Lord.
Amen.

Our Lady and all the saints, pray for us

 **Notes**

What is meant by a 'virtue'? A virtue is an interior disposition, a positive habit, a passion that has been placed at the service of the good (*YOUCAT, 299)

* YOUCAT is the Youth Catechism of the Catholic Church

Signpost
This session looked at the idea of holiness, what can initially seem to be an impossible task yet is one to which we are called. The next session will look at the life of one of our four saints - St Gianna Molla, whose children and husband all attended the ceremony at the Vatican where she was made a saint (canonised).

Sparks of Light

Prudence: St Gianna Molla

Biography
Name: Saint Gianna Molla
Born: 4 October 1922 (Feast of St Francis of Assisi) in Milan
Died: 28 April 1962
Year of beatification: 1994 (The Year of the Family)
Year of canonisation: 2004 (16 May)
Feast Day: 28 April

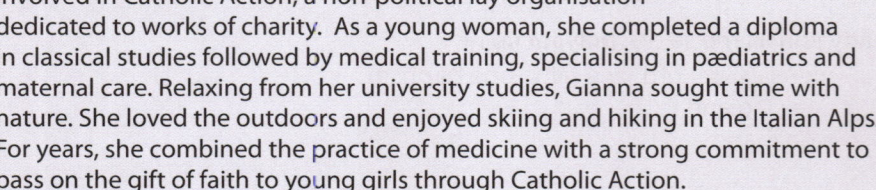

From an early age Giovanna (Gianna) Francesca Beretta was involved in Catholic Action, a non-political lay organisation dedicated to works of charity. As a young woman, she completed a diploma in classical studies followed by medical training, specialising in pædiatrics and maternal care. Relaxing from her university studies, Gianna sought time with nature. She loved the outdoors and enjoyed skiing and hiking in the Italian Alps. For years, she combined the practice of medicine with a strong commitment to pass on the gift of faith to young girls through Catholic Action.

Eventually, Gianna's open, effusive personality caught the attention of Pietro Molla, a mechanical engineer working in management at the nearby Saffa Company. He recounted that it was her joy that attracted him, she was neither gossipy nor chatty – a woman of few words yet deep wisdom that comes from prayer and contemplation before the Lord. Letters from the time of their courtship and engagement brimmed with excitement of a life together under the guidance of the Holy Spirit. Thanking Pietro for the gift of her engagement ring, Gianna wrote of her desire to be a 'valiant woman... doing her husband good and not harm' (Proverbs 31:10, 12). 'I have so much trust in the Lord and I am certain he will help me be a worthy spouse to you.' (St. Gianna Molla, page 57)

Gianna and Pietro's commitment of love, made on their wedding day in 1954, underpinned their daily living. While Gianna continued her charitable works, they were keen to become 'collaborators of God in creation' and together they welcomed the births of their children. Gianna gladly assumed the role of a 'working mum'. She was carrying their fourth child when doctors discovered a fibroma in her uterus. Fully aware of the risk to her own life, she carried on with the pregnancy. A few days before her daughter was born, Gianna said to her husband: 'if you must decide between me and the child, do not hesitate. Choose the child - I insist on it. Save the baby.' Sadly, a fatal infection took her life a week after the delivery.

Beatified by John Paul II, Gianna became the first married laywoman to be canonised. Present for this great occasion were her husband and three surviving children.

Sparks of Light

session two

Opening Prayers
Taken from St Paul's letter to the Ephesians 4:1-15

Leader: Lord, we humbly ask that we be made worthy
of the life to which you have called us,
grant us humility and gentleness,
help us to bear with one another in love,
making every effort to maintain
the unity of the Spirit in the bond of peace.

Group: There is one body and one Spirit,
there is one Lord, one faith, one baptism,
one God and Father of all,
who is above all and through all and in all.

Leader: Each of us was given grace
according to the measure of Christ's gift.

Group: The gifts he gave were that some would be apostles,
some prophets, some evangelists,
some pastors and teachers,
to equip the saints for the work of ministry,
for building up the body of Christ,

Leader: until all of us come to the unity of the faith
and of the knowledge of the Son of God,
to maturity, to the measure of the full stature of Christ.

Group: Grant that we no longer be children,
but speaking the truth in love,
may we grow up in every way into him
who is the head, into Christ. Amen.

As we come together let us, either aloud or in the silence of our hearts, give thanks and praise to the Lord for all the things we have accomplished, the joys experienced, graces received and people met over the past week. Let us also remember all those in need of our prayers.

Sparks of Light

Introduction to Reading of Scripture
Let us pray with great confidence, with confidence based upon the goodness and infinite generosity of God and upon the promises of Jesus Christ. God is a spring of living water which flows unceasingly into the hearts of those who pray.

St Louis de Montfort (1673-1716)

Explore the Scriptures Ephesians 1:3-14
Blessed be the God and Father of our Lord Jesus Christ, who has blessed us in Christ with every spiritual blessing in the heavenly places, just as he chose us in Christ before the foundation of the world to be holy and blameless before him in love. He destined us for adoption as his children through Jesus Christ, according to the good pleasure of his will, to the praise of his glorious grace that he freely bestowed on us in the Beloved. In him we have redemption through his blood, the forgiveness of our trespasses, according to the riches of his grace that he lavished on us. With all wisdom and insight he has made known to us the mystery of his will, according to his good pleasure that he set forth in Christ, as a plan for the fullness of time, to gather up all things in him, things in heaven and things on earth. In Christ we have also obtained an inheritance, having been destined according to the purpose of him who accomplishes all things according to his counsel and will, so that we, who were the first to set our hope on Christ, might live for the praise of his glory. In him you also, when you had heard the word of truth, the gospel of your salvation, and had believed in him, were marked with the seal of the promised Holy Spirit; this is the pledge of our inheritance towards redemption as God's own people, to the praise of his glory.

Please take a few moments in silence to reflect on the passage, then share a word or phrase that has struck you. Pause to think about what others have said then after a second reading of the passage you may wish to share a further thought.

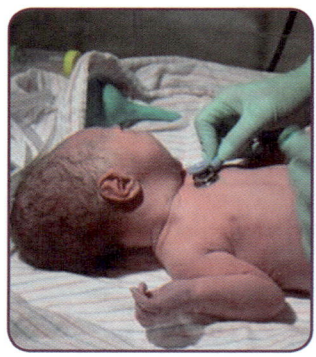  

Sparks of Light

Reflection

A recent news article recounted the story of a young expectant mother confronted with a potentially life threatening tumour growing on her heart. Doctors put forward various options to diffuse this 'ticking time-bomb' but the young mother-to-be chose to postpone any surgery until her unborn child was closer to term. In her words, 'I wanted him to have a chance to survive before me.'

Although the article did not disclose the young woman's family background or faith tradition, her heroic decision echoed that of another young mother, Gianna Molla. Many may wonder why Blessed Pope John Paul II chose to canonise Gianna in the concluding years of the twentieth century? Was it solely the selfless act that tragically took her life or was there more?

On the surface, Gianna's life does not seem appreciably different from others living at that time. However, having grown up in a family of strong faith and with maturity well beyond her years, she soon saw her entire life through the prism of that faith. For a time, she seriously considered becoming a medical missionary and following in the footsteps of her brother, a Capuchin priest working in Brazil but, after prayerful consideration, she determined that her lack of physical stamina was a sign to set aside this idea – that this was not the road God had called her to live.

Building on the cornerstones of her daily life: prayer and Holy Mass, Gianna sought to live the gospel message in the world - in Christ's vineyard. Besides her charitable work among the poor through the St Vincent de Paul Society, she was a devoted leader of Catholic Action with responsibility for the formation of youth. As a highly trained, medical doctor, Gianna viewed her physician's work as a matter of both body and soul. Encouraging her colleagues not to forget the patient's soul, she reminded them that these two are separate entities but united. She wrote: 'God so inserted the divine into the human that everything we do assumes greater value.' Gianna meditated long and prayerfully on God's will for her. 'What is a vocation' she wrote: 'It is a gift from God- it comes from God Himself! We should enter onto the path that God wills for us not by "forcing the door," but when God wills and as God wills.' Gianna believed she was called to marriage and family life and she waited patiently for God's will to be revealed. (St. Gianna Molla, page 8)

In Gianna we have the example of an intellectually gifted woman who could have done anything with her life. After discerning a possible missionary vocation and embarking on a career as a doctor, Gianna Molla, this prudent woman, found her path to holiness as a wife and mother. Illuminated and guided by the light of Christ she loved life and lived it fully. Prudence was not something she fell into but came from her repeated search for the will of God. Her final decision and act was to save the life of her unborn child, she would not have had it any other way.

Sparks of Light

When making a decision it would be sensible to take your time and to consult the experts, however, the right decison can sometimes be what is not commonly-held, comfortable or easy. How can I ensure that the 'right' way takes presedence over the easy way? How am I able to achieve good and avoid evil in my decision-making?

Closing Prayers
You may wish to end this session with some different prayers, the Our Father or silent reflection.

Loving Father,
grant us the strength to flee from temptation
even when it means exile and poverty.
Help us, we pray, to not only know what is right,
but give us also the determination and confidence to do it.
We ask this through your Son, Jesus Christ,
who lives and reigns with you and the Holy Spirit,
one God, for ever and ever.
Amen.

St Gianna Molla, pray for us
Our Lady and all the saints, pray for us

Notes

Prudence is a virtue which helps us to distinguish what is essential from what is non-essential, to set the right goals and to choose the best means of attaining them (YOUCAT, 301)

Signpost
This session explored the human (cardinal) virtue of prudence though the life of St Gianna Molla a young mother who died for her child and who lived a life of great love. Next session we will look at St David Roldán-Lara, a devoted and hard-working son, who died for his faith in a time of great persecution - the 1920s Mexican 'Cristero War'.

Sparks of Light

'ICONOSTASIS' AD 1–500

1. St Augustine of Hippo (died 430); 2. St Ambrose of Milan (340); 3. St Pope Leo the Great (461); 4. St Jerome (420); 5. St Basil the Great (379); 6. St Patrick (493); 7. St Alban (209 or c.251 or 304); 8. St Cyprian (258); 9. St Frumentius (c.383); 10. St Martin of Tours (397); 11. St John Chrysostom (407); 12. St Blaise (316); 13. St Anthony the Great (356); 14. St Clement of Alexandria (c.215); 15: Madonna and Child; 16. The Last Supper

Justice: St David Roldán-Lara

Biography
Name: Saint David Roldán-Lara
Born: 2 March 1902 in Chalchihuites, Mexico
Died: 15 August 1926
Year of beatification: 1992 (23 November)
Year of canonisation: 2000 (21 May)
Feast Day: 21 May

David's father died when he was only a year old. He entered the seminary at Durango when very young, but left to help support his family by working as a miner – where he earned a reputation for kindness, honesty and hard work. Owing to the economic hardship endured by his family, David never returned to the seminary and remained a layman, ever the good son to his mother and 'father' to his brothers. He served the Church through his work with Fr (Saint) Luis Batiz in his local parish. David joined Catholic Action (ACJM) and served as its president in 1925. He was named as vice-president of the National League for the Defence of Religious Liberty (LNDLR) organizing peaceful resistance to the socialist government's anti-religion laws through petitions and demonstrations.

On 15 August 1926, a group of soldiers gathered up the LNDLR officers and announced they were taking them to the state capital to explain their position. Despite the association's 'No to violence', David and his companions, Manuel Morales and Salvador Lara, were falsely accused, along with Fr Luis Batiz, of plotting armed revolt against the government. After leaving town, the soldiers stopped the cars and along with the others in the car, David was offered his freedom if he would recognise the legitimacy of Calles' anti-religious government; he declined. With the cry of 'Viva Cristo Rey and the Virgin of Guadalupe!' on his lips the firing squad cut short his life, he was just 24 years old. His family waited in heavy rain and strong winds before burying him, fearing the arrival of General Eulogio Ortiz, who had intended to display the bodies as a warning to others.

St David was canonised by Blessed John Paul II on 21 May 2000 in the presence of thousands of Mexicans gathered in St Peter's Square together with his 24 companion martyrs from the Cristero War.

session three

Opening prayer
Taken from Psalm 37(36):1-6, 27-28, 37-38

Leader: Do not fret because of the wicked;
do not be envious of wrongdoers,
for they will soon fade like the grass,
and wither like the green herb.

Group: Trust in the Lord, and do good;
so you will live in the land, and enjoy security.
Take delight in the Lord,
and he will give you the desires of your heart.

Leader: Commit your way to the Lord;
trust in him, and he will act.
He will make your vindication shine like the light,
and the justice of your cause like the noonday.

Group: Depart from evil, and do good;
so you shall abide for ever.
For the Lord loves justice;
he will not forsake his faithful ones.

Leader: Mark the blameless, and behold the upright,
for there is posterity for the peaceable.
But transgressors shall be altogether destroyed;
the posterity of the wicked shall be cut off.

All: Glory be to the Father, and to the Son and to the Holy Spirit. As it was in the beginning, is now, and ever shall be, world without end. Amen.

As we come together let us, either aloud or in the silence of our hearts, give thanks and praise to the Lord for all the things we have accomplished, the joys experienced, graces received and people met over the past week. Let us also remember all those in need of our prayers.

Sparks of Light

Introduction to Reading of Scripture
Let us listen carefully to the Word of the Lord,
and attend to it with the ear of our hearts.
Let us welcome it, and faithfully put it into practice.
St. Benedict of Nursia (c.480-c.547) adapted

Explore the Scriptures 2 Maccabees 6:18-20, 21-28, 31
Eleazar, one of the scribes in high position, a man now advanced in age and of noble presence, was being forced to open his mouth to eat swine's flesh. But he, welcoming death with honour rather than life with pollution, went up to the rack of his own accord, spitting out the flesh. Those who were in charge of that unlawful sacrifice took the man aside because of their long acquaintance with him, and privately urged him to bring meat of his own providing, proper for him to use, and to pretend that he was eating the flesh of the sacrificial meal that had been commanded by the king, so that by doing this he might be saved from death, and be treated kindly on account of his old friendship with them. But making a high resolve, worthy of his years and the dignity of his old age and the grey hairs that he had reached with distinction and his excellent life even from childhood, and moreover according to the holy God-given law, he declared himself quickly, telling them to send him to Hades.

'Such pretence is not worthy of our time of life,' he said, 'for many of the young might suppose that Eleazar in his ninetieth year had gone over to an alien religion, and through my pretence, for the sake of living a brief moment longer, they would be led astray because of me, while I defile and disgrace my old age. Even if for the present I would avoid the punishment of mortals, yet whether I live or die I will not escape the hands of the Almighty. Therefore, by bravely giving up my life now, I will show myself worthy of my old age and leave to the young a noble example of how to die a good death willingly and nobly for the revered and holy laws. In my soul I am glad to suffer these things because I fear him.' So

in this way he died, leaving in his death an example of nobility and a memorial of courage, not only to the young but to the great body of his nation.

Please take a few moments in silence to reflect on the passage, then share a word or phrase that has struck you. Pause to think about what others have said then after a second reading of the passage you may wish to share a further thought.

Reflection

One of the greatest threats to this century is that of terrorism. Improvements in technology combined with the willingness of people to die in order to inflict damage on their enemies have made the world a dangerous place. When people think martyr, thoughts often turn to suicide bombers, those who kill for a cause giving up their own life into the bargain. Christian martyrdom is an altogether different thing. It seeks not to harm but to demonstrate love. It is not selfish but selfless. It ennobles the one dying for Christ and inspires those who encounter them. In the manner of his death, St Gregory Nazianzen calls Eleazar 'the greatest of all those who suffered before the coming of Christ; as Stephen is first among those who endure suffering after Christ'.

As Eleazar and St Stephen died rather than giving up their faith, other Christian martyrs such as David Roldán-Lara, his cousin Salvador, and countless more have done the same over the centuries. The stories of Eleazar, St Stephen and St David Roldán-Lara tell of heroic resistance to tyranny. St Stephen, St David and Eleazar were given opportunities to deny their faith in return for their lives, however, all three died with the desire to serve God in their hearts, died as 'memorials of courage'. Thanks be to God, not all of us are called to die for our faith. Each of us is, however, called to serve God – such service is to be characterised by love and is brought about by dying to ourselves, our pride and our desires.

One of the more striking moments during Holy Week is the washing of the feet, the Mandatum – Christ's command to serve (John 13:34). Christ set the example for his followers: be the one who serves, avoid the conceit of pride. Value yourself by all means but value others and humbly seek to serve them with love. We followers of Christ are called to be constant and firm in our desire to give God and neighbour their due. To do this, to 'die for God' in the context of our daily lives, we require what St David recognised as God's grace. To have the strength to face persecution and trouble we need God – it is impossible to rely simply and solely on your own power and wits. Living for others and for God means making sacrifices, it means tolerating life's small hurts. Every stage of life has its 'givings' and 'dyings' and it is through these that we grow closer to Christ.

The Catechism tells us that a key component of justice is the determination to give their due to God and neighbour. What do I consider to be God's due? What about my neighbours'? How can I serve both God and society?

Closing Prayers
You may wish to end this session with some different prayers, the Our Father or silent reflection.

Almighty God,
you who are faithful, true and righteous in all your ways;
Teach us to choose what is right,
and stand against that which is evil.
Teach us to love justice and mercy,
and stand against oppression and exploitation.
Show us where we are indifferent to injustice.
Empower us with your spirit,
so we may have the courage and determination to do your will.
We trust you because you are Lord,
and your love endures forever.
Amen.

St David Roldán-Lara, pray for us
St Gianna Molla, pray for us
Our Lady and all the saints, pray for us

Notes

Justice is a virtue which is manifested when we make sure to give to God and to one's neighbour what is due to them (YOUCAT, 302).

Signpost

This session explored the virtue of justice though the life and death of St David Roldán-Lara, a hard-working young man, who served both his family and the Church and who was martyred during the 'Cristero War'. Next session we will look at St Josephine Bakhita, a young girl taken into slavery who was able to keep living love and forgiveness.

Sparks of Light

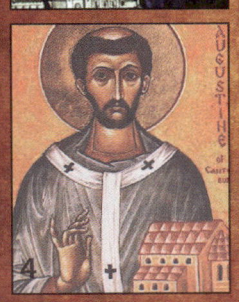

'ICONOSTASIS' AD500–1000

1. St Benedict of Nursia (died 547); 2. St Columba (597); 3. St Werburga (699); 4. St Augustine of Canterbury (604); 5. St Scholastica (547); 6. St David (601); 7. St Bede (735); 8. St Cyril (c.826) and St Methodius (815); 9. St Isidore of Seville (636); 10. St Wenceslaus (935); 11. St Alcuin of York (804); 12. St Boniface (755); 13. St Chad (672); 14. St John of Damascus (749); 15: Madonna and Child; 16. The Last Supper

Fortitude: St Josephine Bakhita

Biography
Name: Saint Josephine Bakhita
Born: c.1869 in Olgossa, Darfur, Sudan
Died: 8 February 1947
Year of beatification: 1992 (17 May)
Year of canonisation: 2000 (1 October)
Feast Day: 8 February

St Josephine Bakhita, also known as 'Mother Moretta' (our Black Mother) bore 144 physical scars throughout her life which were received after she was kidnapped at the age of nine and sold into slavery. Such was the trauma experienced that she forgot her birth name and her kidnappers gave her the name Bakhita meaning 'fortunate'. Flogging and maltreatment were part of her daily life. She experienced the moral and physical humiliations associated with slavery.

It was only in 1882 that her suffering was alleviated after she was bought for the Italian Consul. This event was to transform her life. In this family and, subsequently in a second Italian home, she received from her masters, kindness, respect, peace and joy. Josephine came to discover love in a profound way even though at first she was unable to name its source.

A change in her owner's circumstances meant that she was entrusted to the Canossian Sisters of the Institute of the Catechumens in Venice. It was there that Bakhita came to know about God whom, 'she had experienced in her heart without knowing who He was' since she was a child. She was received into the Catholic Church in 1890, joining the sisters and making final profession in 1896.

The next fifty years of her life were spent witnessing to God's love through cooking, sewing, embroidery and attending to the door. When she was on door duty, she would gently lay her hands on the heads of the children who attended the nearby school and caress them. Her voice was pleasing to the little ones, comforting to the poor and suffering. She was a source of encouragement. Her constant smile won people's hearts, as did her humility and simplicity.

As she grew older she experienced long, painful years of sickness, but she continued to persevere in hope, constantly choosing the good. When visited and asked how she was, she'd respond: 'As the Master desires'. During her last days she relived the painful days of her slavery and more than once begged: 'Please, loosen the chains… they are heavy!' Surrounded by the sisters, she died on 8 February 1947.

session four

Opening prayer
Taken from Psalm 118(117): 1-15

Leader: Give thanks to the Lord for he is good,
for his faithful love endures for ever.

Group: Let the House of Israel say, 'His faithful love endures for ever.'
Let the House of Aaron say, 'His faithful love endures for ever.'
Let those who fear the Lord say, 'His faithful love endures for ever.'

Leader: In my distress I called to the Lord,
he heard me and brought me relief.

Group: With the Lord on my side I fear nothing;
what can human beings do to me?
With the Lord on my side as my help, I gloat over my enemies.

Leader: It is better to take refuge in the Lord than to rely on human beings;
better to take refuge in the Lord than to rely on princes.

Group: Nations were swarming around me,
in the name of the Lord I cut them down;
they swarmed around me, pressing upon me,
in the name of the Lord I cut them down.
They swarmed around me like bees,
they flared up like a brushwood fire,
in the name of the Lord I cut them down.

Leader: I was pushed hard, to make me fall, but the Lord came to my help.

Group: The Lord is my strength and my song, he has been my Saviour.
Shouts of joy and salvation, in the tents of the upright,
'The Lord's right hand is triumphant.'

All: Glory be to the Father, and to the Son and to the Holy Spirit. As it was in the beginning, is now, and ever shall be, world without end. Amen.

As we come together let us, either aloud or in the silence of our hearts, give thanks and praise to the Lord for all the things we have accomplished, the joys experienced, graces received and people met over the past week. Let us also remember all those in need of our prayers.

Sparks of Light

Introduction to Reading of Scripture
Let us pray with great confidence, with confidence based upon the goodness and infinite generosity of God and upon the promises of Jesus Christ. God is a spring of living water which flows unceasingly into the hearts of those who pray.

St Louis de Montfort (1673-1716)

Explore the Scriptures John 16:24-33
In all truth I tell you, anything you ask from the Father he will grant in my name. Until now you have not asked anything in my name. Ask and you will receive, and so your joy will be complete. I have been telling you these things in veiled language. The hour is coming when I shall no longer speak to you in veiled language but tell you about the Father in plain words. When that day comes you will ask in my name; and I do not say that I shall pray to the Father for you, because the Father himself loves you for loving me, and believing that I came from God. I came from the Father and have come into the world and now I am leaving the world to go to the Father.'

His disciples said, 'Now you are speaking plainly and not using veiled language. Now we see that you know everything and need not wait for questions to be put into words; because of this we believe that you came from God.'

Jesus answered them: 'Do you believe at last? Listen; the time will come - indeed it has come already - when you are going to be scattered, each going his own way and leaving me alone. And yet I am not alone, because the Father is with me. I have told you all this so that you may find peace in me. In the world you will have hardship, but be courageous: I have conquered the world.'

Please take a few moments in silence to reflect on the passage, then share a word or phrase that has struck you. Pause to think about what others have said then after a second reading of the passage you may wish to share a further thought.

Reflection
One of the things that the Lord invites us to do during Lent is to let go of past hurts and hand them over to him for his healing touch so that we can become whole again. A desire to receive his healing, his forgiveness and to forgive others is essential to the work of grace. With the Lord's help, as the life and example of St Josephine Bakhita teaches, we will be able to do day-by-day what others regard impossible .

It would have been easy for St Josephine to have let her early life shape her in a way that meant she was embittered and closed off to others, especially from friendship and love. Despite everything that she endured she broke the cycle of sin and pain choosing to let go and begin a new life with God as her spiritual

Master. Pope Benedict XVI highlighted in *Spe Salvi* (*In Hope we are Saved*) that, she 'helps us understand what it means to have a real encounter with this God for the first time,' (SS, 3) and to experience God's transforming power.

As Christians we are called to witness daily to someone beyond ourselves, whose strength becomes our strength, especially when people hurt us and things don't go as we had hoped. Josephine sought and received the grace to let her ongoing relationship with Christ shape her past, present and future, freeing her from all that enslaved her.

Through knowledge of Christ Josephine was 'redeemed', both in terms of being freed from actual slavery, but also interiorly she discovered what it means to live as a free child of God. Her physical scars did not hinder her because she lived the reality that God's power is greater than every evil, every sin. Josephine's life teaches us that although the road to holiness is often marked by times of intense suffering, this is not the end of the story. With God's grace, if we surrender all that we are to him, we can be healed, reconciled and forgiven, and in turn can be a signpost for others to the source of those gifts. We can come to understand that trials can bring blessing with God's help.

One of the things that marked Josephine's life was that her sanctity was not proved in a solitary act but it was lived daily. From her conversion she chose to embrace goodness, love, joy and humility. Each day of her religious life she strived to open the door with smile and offer a comforting word to visitors. She did the same to witness to God's love through all her daily activities. Convent life must have brought its own challenges and yet she remained constant, handing over all that she was to Jesus.

We are invited to do the same, to let go and live in expectant hope, remaining constant whatever befalls us, fixing our gaze on our heavenly Master in whom we find everything.

Sparks of Light

If I had experienced all that St Josephine had experienced as a slave would I have responded in the same way as her, or instead succumbed to temptation becoming embittered, angry and self-pitying? Can I identify any good, any blessings, that have come out of awful experiences in my life? Who and what sustains me during life's trials?

Closing Prayers
You may wish to end this session with some different prayers, the Our Father or silent reflection.

Loving Father help us to seek and find our strength in you,
give us the grace to resist temptation and to seek and do good,
preserve us in all the trials that we face;
help us to imitate the life of St Josephine Bakhita so that we too may bear all that we face with joy and constancy,
transforming all that we experience in life into blessing.
Amen.

St Josephine Bakhita, pray for us
St David Roldán-Lara, pray for us
St Gianna Molla, pray for us
Our Lady and all the saints, pray for us

 **Notes**

Fortitude is the moral virtue that ensures firmness in difficulties and constancy in the pursuit of the good. It strengthens the resolve to resist temptations and to overcome obstacles in the moral life (CCC, 1808)

Signpost
This session explored the virtue of fortitude though the life of St Josephine Bakhita who, with God's grace, overcame many trials and witnessed to the reality of God's love and forgiveness. Next session we will look at Blessed Pier Giorgio Frassati, a young man, who rejected the path chosen for him instead living his life in the service of the poor.

Sparks of Light

'ICONOSTASIS' AD 1000–1500

1. St Catherine of Siena (died 1380); 2. St Francis of Assisi (1226); 3. St Dominic de Guzmán (1221); 4. St Julian of Norwich (1342); 5. St Thomas Aquinas (1274); 6. St Bridget of Sweden (1373); 7. St Bonaventure (1274); 8. St Thomas à Becket (1170); 9. St Richard of Chichester (1253); 10. St Hildegard of Bingen (1179); 11. St Edward the Confessor (1066); 12. St Bernard of Clairvaux (1153); 13. St Rita of Cascia (1457); 14. St Anselm of Canterbury (1109); 15: Nativity; 16. The Last Supper

Temperance: Bl Pier Giorgio Frassati

Biography
Name: Blessed Pier Giorgio Frassati
Born: 6 April 1901 in Turin, Italy
Died: 4 July 1925
Year of beatification: 1990 (20 May)
Year of canonisation: yet to occur
Feast Day: 4 July

Pier Giorgio Frassati was born at the start of the twentieth century in the northern Italian city of Torino (in English, Turin). At that time, FIAT and Lancia were fast becoming national and indeed internationally known carmakers and hundreds of thousands of southern Italians were streaming into the area in search of jobs in the growing automotive industry. At the same time, this one time capital of Italy was attracting artists keen to participate in the Art Nouveau movement.

In many ways, this was Frassatti's world. Although he was born into a Catholic family, devotion was not particularly important to either of his parents. His mother, Adelaide was an accomplished painter and his father, Alfredo, an agnostic, owned and edited the well-known *La Stampa* newspaper. An influential businessman, Alfredo was appointed a senator and he also served as ambassador to Germany in 1921-1923. While his business interests kept him away from home much of the time, he provided wealth and status for his family who also enjoyed the use of their mother's family villa at Pollone.

Pier Giorgio and his younger sister Luciana were privately tutored in their early years. However, much to his parents' chagrin (who hoped that he would one day be a Director of *La Stampa*), Pier Giorgio did not excel academically and he was sent off to the Jesuit school, Instituto Social. There, despite the initial resistance of his mother, Pier Giorgio began regularly to partake of the sacraments. As well, those two years also enabled him to deepen his faith through prayer and to turn more of his attention to those in need.

While war temporarily disrupted his formal studies, the adolescent Pier Giorgio sought out small ways of helping those struggling to cope with the loss of family members, often giving his own overcoat or bus fare to the less fortunate. It was also during this time that ideological differences led to the widening of the gulf between his parents and himself. Pier Giorgio showed little interest in managing the family holdings instead he scaled the nearby Alps: mountain climbing in summer, and skiing the winter months. He prayed the rosary daily and actively supported the

Sparks of Light

session five

> Popular Party in their efforts to improve the lot of workers. Most notably, he quietly and continuously reached out to the poor, sharing what little he received from his family and whatever he could garner from friends. He would run home or sit in third class on the train to have funds for those in great need.
>
> Although not a particularly gifted student, he chose a rigorous mining engineering programme. Having turned aside any thoughts of a priestly vocation or even the possibility of marriage to a young woman who did not 'measure up' in the eyes of his mother, Pier Giorgio hoped to work among miners. However, with just two exams remaining, he was summoned to work at *La Stampa*. Always hoping to please his papa, he accepted.
>
> Sadly, poliomyelitis had already taken hold and this spirited young man died just a few weeks later. Bewildering his family, his funeral procession drew large crowds of poor people.

Opening prayer
Taken from Psalm 37(36):7-11, 23-24

Leader: Be still before the Lord, and wait patiently for him;
do not fret over those who prosper in their way,
over those who carry out evil devices.

Group: Refrain from anger, and forsake wrath.
Do not fret – it leads only to evil.
For the wicked shall be cut off,
but those who wait for the Lord shall inherit the land.

Leader: Yet a little while, and the wicked will be no more;
though you look diligently for their place, they will not be there.
But the meek shall inherit the land,
and delight in abundant prosperity.

Group: Our steps are made firm by the Lord,
when he delights in our way;
though we stumble, we shall not fall headlong,
for the Lord holds us by the hand.

All: Glory be to the Father, and to the Son and to the Holy Spirit. As it was in the beginning, is now, and ever shall be, world without end. Amen.

Sparks of Light

As we come together let us, either aloud or in the silence of our hearts, give thanks and praise to the Lord for all the things we have accomplished, the joys experienced, graces received and people met over the past week. Let us also remember all those in need of our prayers.

Introduction to Reading of Scripture
Our hearts were made for You, O Lord,
and they are restless until they rest in you.

St Augustine of Hippo (354-430)

Explore the Scriptures Matthew 6:1-6, 16-18
Beware of practising your piety before others in order to be seen by them; for then you have no reward from your Father in heaven.

So whenever you give alms, do not sound a trumpet before you, as the hypocrites do in the synagogues and in the streets, so that they may be praised by others. Truly I tell you, they have received their reward. But when you give alms, do not let your left hand know what your right hand is doing, so that your alms may be done in secret; and your Father who sees in secret will reward you.

And whenever you pray, do not be like the hypocrites; for they love to stand and pray in the synagogues and at the street corners, so that they may be seen by others. Truly I tell you, they have received their reward. But whenever you pray, go into your room and shut the door and pray to your Father who is in secret; and your Father who sees in secret will reward you.

And whenever you fast, do not look dismal, like the hypocrites, for they disfigure their faces so as to show others that they are fasting. Truly I tell you, they have received their reward. But when you fast, put oil on your head and wash your face, so that your fasting may be seen not by others but by your Father who is in secret; and your Father who sees in secret will reward you.

Please take a few moments in silence to reflect on the passage, then share a word or phrase that has struck you. Pause to think about what others have said then after a second reading of the passage you may wish to share a further thought.

Reflection
How often do we hear that we are living in uncertain times and how particularly challenging it is for young people today. The late Blessed Pope John Paul II did not live to see the crisis in the Eurozone, the widespread political unrest in the Middle East or to read about the massive numbers of young people struggling to find employment throughout the world. Yet, he chose to beatify a young man who experienced similarly trying times. As a teenager living in Italy during the

years of the Great War (1914-18), Blessed Pier Giorgio Frassati saw firsthand its devastating impact on families, in particular the poor. When he entered university, it was expected that he become politically active and there he chose to join the *Cesare Balbo*, the Catholic Club. Given his strength and enthusiasm, he was soon waving their flag at demonstrations and speaking out against the growing threat of Mussolini's fascist regime.

Rarely do we hear of a young person of such profound and fervent faith coming from a family where it was not at all encouraged. Perhaps this was another reason why our late Holy Father brought this young man to our attention. Although Pier Giorgio had been given every advantage: social status, financial security and material comforts, he refused to use them for his own gain. On the contrary, his faith, initially fostered by the Jesuits in high school, became the lens through which he viewed the world. While prayer and the Eucharist anchored each day, an unselfish kindness permeated his daily activities. Growing up, he was continually striving to share not only his worldly possessions but also his presence. From a young age he reached out, befriending those in need, seeking those little ways in which he could share their plight and to alleviate their suffering. Seeing the face of Christ in those that he met, Pier Giorgio sought out the places they lived, where they worked. It was while working with the poor that he contracted polio which quickly took his life.

Doing without so that others may have was second nature to Pier Giorgio. Living a frugal life, a life of temperance and moderation, is often considered joyless; associated with the 'Victorian era' and not contemporary living. The life of Blessed Pier Giorgio, however, shows temperance as something radical - a source of great joy. Instead of accepting the clear path of wealth and advantage offered by his family he moderated his own needs and was thereby able to relieve the suffering of many. Indeed when he died, his family were surprised at the number of poor and homeless who turned out to pay their respects to Pier Giorgio. Temperance

Sparks of Light

freed him to be what God had called him to be, who he wanted to be and not what others would have had him be.

Pier Giorgio was born into wealth but lived charity. What could I do without, so that others may have a little? Much of what Pier Giorgio did was in quiet and unseen. Am I capable of doing good without acknowledgement?

Closing Prayers
You may wish to end this session with some different prayers or silent reflection.

Heavenly Father,
give us the courage to strive for the highest goals,
to flee every temptation to be mediocre.
Enable us to aspire to greatness, as Pier Giorgio did,
and to open our hearts in joy to your call to holiness.
Free us from the fear of failure and grant
us the graces we ask You through Pier Giorgio's intercession,
by the merits of Our Lord Jesus Christ.
Amen.

Blessed Pier Giorgio Frassati, pray for us
St Josephine Bakhita, pray for us
St David Roldán-Lara, pray for us
St Gianna Molla, pray for us
Our Lady and all the saints, pray for us

Notes

Temperence or moderation is the virtue that moderates the attraction of pleasures and provides balance in the use of created goods. It ensures that the will masters our instincts and is directed to what is good (CCC, 1809)

Signpost
This session explored the virtue of temperance though the life of Blessed Pier Giorgio Frassati. For him temperance was not a negative thing but something radical that allowed him to live for others as Christ did. Next session we will look at all of the virtues and our own pilgrim journey to God.

'ICONOSTASIS' AD 1500-2000

1. St Thomas More (died 1535); 2. St Maria Goretti (1902); 3. St John Bosco (1888); 4. St Martin de Porres (1639); 5. St Edith Stein (1942); 6. St Ignatius Loyola (1556); 7. St John Southworth (1654); 8. St Katherine Drexel (1955); 9. St Bernadette (1879); 10. St Jean Vianney (1859); 11. St Philip Howard (1595); 12. St Aloysius Gonzaga (1591); 13. St Francis Cabrini (1917); 14. St Charles Borromeo (1584); 15: Madonna and Child; 16. The Last Supper

Virtuous living

session six

Opening prayer
Taken from Psalm 36 (35):5-10

Leader: Your steadfast love, O Lord,
extends to the heavens,
your faithfulness to the clouds.

Group: Your righteousness is like the mighty mountains,
your judgements are like the great deep;
you save humans and animals alike, O Lord.

Leader: How precious is your steadfast love, O God!
All people may take refuge in the shadow of your wings.

Group: They feast on the abundance of your house,
and you give them drink from the river of your delights.

Leader: For with you is the fountain of life;
in your light we see light.

Group: O continue your steadfast love to those who know you,
and your salvation to the upright of heart!

All: Glory be to the Father, and to the Son and to the Holy Spirit. As it was in the beginning, is now, and ever shall be, world without end. Amen.

As we come together let us, either aloud or in the silence of our hearts, give thanks and praise to the Lord for all the things we have accomplished, the joys experienced, graces received and people met over the past week. Let us also remember all those in need of our prayers.

Introduction to Reading of Scripture
Let us pray with great confidence, with confidence based upon the goodness and infinite generosity of God and upon the promises of Jesus Christ. God is a spring of living water which flows unceasingly into the hearts of those who pray.

St Louis de Montfort (1673-1716)

Sparks of Light

Explore the Scriptures Philippians 3:10-16, 4:4-9

I want to know Christ and the power of his resurrection and the sharing of his sufferings by becoming like him in his death, if somehow I may attain the resurrection from the dead.

Not that I have already obtained this or have already reached the goal; but I press on to make it my own, because Christ Jesus has made me his own. Beloved, I do not consider that I have made it my own; but this one thing I do: forgetting what lies behind and straining forward to what lies ahead, I press on towards the goal for the prize of the heavenly call of God in Christ Jesus. Let those of us then who are mature be of the same mind; and if you think differently about anything, this too God will reveal to you. Only let us hold fast to what we have attained…

Rejoice in the Lord always; again I will say, Rejoice. Let your gentleness be known to everyone. The Lord is near. Do not worry about anything, but in everything by prayer and supplication with thanksgiving let your requests be made known to God. And the peace of God, which surpasses all understanding, will guard your hearts and your minds in Christ Jesus.

Finally, beloved, whatever is true, whatever is honourable, whatever is just, whatever is pure, whatever is pleasing, whatever is commendable, if there is any excellence and if there is anything worthy of praise, think about these things. Keep on doing the things that you have learned and received and heard and seen in me, and the God of peace will be with you.

Please take a few moments in silence to reflect on the passage, then share a word or phrase that has struck you. Pause to think about what others have said then after a second reading of the passage you may wish to share a further thought.

Reflection

A saint is someone who loves because they have experienced the love of God. A saint is not someone who lives the 'God part' of their life for an hour or even a day each week but one who strives to make every moment, ordinary or extraordinary, in failure and success alike, a moment where God could enter.

When St Thérèse's relics were brought to the United Kingdom a great wave of popular piety was unleashed. Her life was not grand or brash or 'exotic' but was characterised by her 'little way'. Each moment was an opportunity for grace and a chance to demonstrate care and concern. Each moment was for Thérèse, and can be for us, one in which we can give and receive love. This, as the Apostle writes, is the greatest of things (1 Corinthians 13:8-13). Love can be demonstrated through quiet prayer or through actions in the midst of noise and conflict; it is cultivated in a life of virtue. Each moment of the day – if seen as such – is gifted to us so that we can grow closer to God through our choices and our actions. St Augustine puts this wonderfully when he writes:

> To live well is nothing other than to love God with all one's heart, with all one's soul and with all one's efforts; from this it comes about that love is kept whole and uncorrupted (through temperance). No misfortune can disturb it (and this is fortitude). It obeys only God (and this is justice), and is careful in discerning things, so as not to be surprised by deceit or trickery (and this is prudence).

The human virtues of prudence, justice, fortitude and temperance must be practised in order to bear fruit. Their opposites, rashness, injustice, weak-mindedness and greed, distract us from what should be the true focus of our lives. The difficulties we experience and the challenges we face threaten to turn us away from God but again, as St Paul writes, such 'troubles train us for carrying the weight of eternal glory which is out of proportion to all of them' (2 Corinthians 4:17). St Gianna Molla, St David Roldán-Lara, St Josephine Bakhita and Blessed Pier Giorgio Frassati all experienced hardship; they faced it with faith strengthened by prayer and sacrament, by 'training in virtue'.

Whether lay, ordained or religious, married or single, each of our saints show us that all states of life can become, with the action of grace and with commitment and perseverance, ways of sanctification. Our task as twenty-first century Christians is to fix our eyes on Christ, all the while training ourselves to see right, to think right and to act right. Our task is to be like Christ and our path is that of the saints.

The Year of Faith

At a Mass for the 'New Evangelisation' on 16 October 2011, Pope Benedict XVI announced a Year of Faith. The purpose of this Year was to 'give a fresh impetus to the mission of the whole Church to lead human beings out of the wilderness in which they often find themselves to the place of life, friendship with Christ that gives us life in fullness.'

The Year of Faith starts on 11 October 2012, on the 50th anniversary of the opening of the Second Vatican Council and ends on the Solemnity of Christ the King (24 November 2013). It will be an opportunity for growth and mission for us all.

Briefly, which saint has inspired you the most? When have you witnessed holiness in the life of another? When have you felt most holy? In light of all this, what new thing could you do to grow in holiness? To discern your next step you may wish to use the materials offered on pages 60-61.

Closing Prayers
You may wish to end this session with some different prayers or silent reflection.

O Almighty and all-knowing God,
without beginning or end,
who art the giver, preserver, and rewarder of all virtue:
Grant me to stand firm on the solid foundation of faith,
be protected by the invincible shield of hope,
and be adorned by the nuptial garment of charity;
Grant me by justice to obey thee,
by prudence to resist the crafts of the Devil,
by temperance to hold to moderation,
by fortitude to bear adversity with patience;
Amen.

Holy Mary, Mother of God, pray for us
Holy angels of God, pray for us
The Apostles and martyrs, pray for us
All holy men and women, pray for us

Notes

Signpost This session looked at holiness recalling the lives of our four saints through the prism of the human (cardinal) virtues of prudence, justice, fortitude and temperance. The next season of faith-sharing will explore what is meant by the 'new evangelisation', how sharing our faith with others is an act of deep love and service to the world at large.

Sparks of Light

Christ Enthroned, Holy Souls Chapel (Westminster Cathedral)

Sparks of Light

Daily Prayer
Sunday to Saturday

The daily prayers on the following pages are drawn from the Divine Office (Liturgy of the Hours). Each day contains a hymn, a Scripture reading, a psalm or Old Testament canticle and a selection of prayers taken from the feast of All Saints and the various Commons of Apostles, Martyrs, Men Saints and Women Saints.

Together with the Mass, the Divine Office (Liturgy of the Hours) constitutes the official public prayer life of the Church. It is celebrated, under different names, in both the Eastern and Western Churches. The Divine Office is intended to be read communally but here we invite you to use it as a personal daily prayer.

'The Office is... the prayer not only of the clergy but of the whole People of God.' *Apostolic Constitution, Canticum Laudis*

Sunday - All the Saints

Introduction
O God, come to our aid. Lord, make haste to help us.

Glory be to the Father and to the Son and to the Holy Spirit, as it was in the beginning, is now, and ever shall be, world without end. Amen. (Alleluia)

omit Alleluias during Lent

Hymn
O fair is our Lord's own city,
With clearest light abloom,
And full of joy and music,
Where woe can never come.

No guilt or condemnation
Its citizens may know,
None weary is, none anxious,
No head by grief bent low.

The saints and martyrs countless,
Who in this world found woe,
Find there a place and pleasure
The world cannot bestow.

From earth our faces turning
Towards the King of grace,
In prayer let us beseech him
To bring us to that place.

Antiphon
Undying light will shine about your saints, Lord; they will live for ever.

Psalmody
Psalm 112 (113)
Praise, O servants of the Lord,
praise the name of the Lord!
May the name of the Lord be blessed
both now and for evermore!

From the rising of the sun to its setting
praised be the name of the Lord!

High above all nations is the Lord,
above the heavens his glory.
Who is like the Lord, our God,
who has risen on high to his throne
yet stoops from the heights to look down,
to look down upon heaven and earth?

From the dust he lifts up the lowly,
from the dungheap he raises the poor
to set them in the company of princes,
yes, with the princes of his people.
To the childless wife he gives a home
and gladdens her heart with children.

Glory be…

Antiphon
Undying light will shine about your saints, Lord; they will live for ever.

Reading *Hebrews 12:22-24*
What you have come to is Mount Zion and the city of the living God, the heavenly Jerusalem where the millions of angels have entered for the festival with the whole Church in which everyone is a 'first-born son' and a citizen of heaven. You have come to God himself, the supreme Judge, and been placed with spirits of the saints who have been made perfect; and to Jesus, the mediator who brings a new covenant and a blood for purification which pleads more insistently than Abel's.

Short Responsory
℟ The just shall rejoice at the presence of God.
℣ They shall exult and dance for joy.
Glory be…

Benedictus/Magnificat Antiphon
The glorious band of apostles, the noble company of prophets, the white-robed army who shed their blood for Christ and all the saints in heaven together proclaim: We praise you, Holy Trinity, one God.

Benedictus (if said in the morning)
or Magnificat (if said in the evening) -
see inside front cover for these prayers

Intercessions
With so many witnesses in a great cloud on every side of us, we are encouraged to run steadily in the race we have started. We pray to Christ, for he is the author of our faith, and he will bring it to fulfilment:
℟ With all the saints we praise and thank you, Lord.

Lord, you chose the Apostles to be the foundation of your Church – keep us faithful to all that you left in their care.
℟ With all the saints we praise and thank you, Lord.

Your martyrs testified to you, even to the shedding of their blood – make all Christians faithful witnesses to your word.
℟ With all the saints we praise and thank you, Lord.

Welcome our departed brothers and sisters into the company of Mary, Joseph, and all the saints – through their intercession, grant us a place in your kingdom.
℟ With all the saints we praise and thank you, Lord.

Our Father…

Concluding prayer
Almighty, ever-living God,
we are celebrating with joy
the triumph of your grace in all the saints.
With so vast a multitude praying for us,
may we receive from you
the fullness of mercy we have always desired.
We make our prayer through
Christ our Lord.
Amen.

Let us go forward in peace, our eyes upon heaven, the only one goal of our labours.
St Thérèse of Lisieux

Sparks of Light

Monday - Praying for Grace

Introduction
O God, come to our aid. Lord, make haste to help us.

Glory be to the Father and to the Son and to the Holy Spirit, as it was in the beginning, is now, and ever shall be, world without end. Amen. (Alleluia)
omit Alleluias during Lent

Hymn
Come, Holy Spirit, live in us
With God the Father and the Son,
And grant us all the grace we need
To sanctify and make us one.

May mind and tongue made stong in love,
Your praise thoughout the world proclaim,
And may that love within our hearts
Set fire to others with its flame.

Most blessed Trinity of love
For whom the heart of man was made,
To you be praise in timeless song,
And everlasting homage paid.

Antiphon
It is not you who speaks: the Spirit of your Father speaks in you.

Psalmody
Psalm 126 (127)
If the Lord does not build the house,
in vain do its builders labour;
if the Lord does not watch over the city,
in vain do the watchers keep vigil.

In vain is your earlier rising,
your going later to rest,
you who toil for the bread you eat,
when he pours gifts on his beloved while they slumber.

Yes, children are a gift from the Lord,
a blessing, the fruit of the womb.
The sons and daughters of youth
are like arrows in the hand of the warrior.

O the happiness of those
who have filled their quiver with these arrows!
They will have no cause for shame
when they dispute with their foes in the gateways.

Glory be...

Antiphon
It is not you who speaks: the Spirit of your Father speaks in you.

Reading *Philippians 3:7-8*
Because of Christ I have come to consider all of these advantages that I had as disadvantages. Not only that, but I believe that nothing can happen that will outweigh the supreme advantage of knowing Christ Jesus my Lord. For him, I have accepted the loss of everything, and I look on everything as so much rubbish, if only I can have Christ.

Short Responsory
℟ Let the saints rejoice in the Lord.
℣ God has chosen you for his own.
Glory be…

Benedictus/Magnificat Antiphon
The one who lives by the truth comes out into the light, so it may be plainly seen that what they do is done in God.

Benedictus (if said in the morning)
or Magnificat (if said in the evening) -
see inside front cover for these prayers

Intercessions
Let us pray to Christ, the high priest, who was appointed to represent us in our relations with God.

℟ Lord, save your people.

Lord Jesus, in times past you have lighted the way for your people through the wise and holy – may Christians always enjoy this sign of your loving kindness.

℟ Lord, save your people.

You forgave the sins of your people when your holy ones prayed – continually cleanse your Church through their powerful intercession.

℟ Lord, save your people.

In the presence of their brethren, you anointed your holy ones and poured on them your Spirit – fill with your Holy Spirit all those who lead your people.

℟ Lord, save your people.

Our Father…

Concluding prayer
Almighty, ever-living God,
you give the saints to the Church
to show others the way of salvation,
grant that inspired by their example
we may so follow Christ our Master,
that, together with our brethren,
we may come at length into your presence.
We make our prayer through Christ our Lord.
Amen.

Let us go forward in peace, our eyes upon heaven, the only one goal of our labours.
St Thérèse of Lisieux

Sparks of Light

Tuesday - Shining for others

Introduction
O God, come to our aid. Lord, make haste to help us.

Glory be to the Father and to the Son and to the Holy Spirit, as it was in the beginning, is now, and ever shall be, world without end. Amen. (Alleluia)

omit Alleluias during Lent

Hymn
O fathers of our ancient faith,
With all the heav'ns we sing your fame
Whose sound went forth in all the earth
To tell of Christ, and bless his name.

You took the gospel to the poor,
The word of God alight in you,
Which in our day is told again:
That timeless word, for ever new.

You told of God who died for us
And out of death triumphant rose,
Who gave the truth that made us free,
And changeless through the ages goes.

Praise Father, Son and Holy Ghost
Whose gift is faith that never dies:
A light in darkness now, until
The day-star in our hearts arise.

Antiphon
Go, preach the Good News of the kingdom: you received without cost; give without charge.

Psalmody

Psalm 46 (47)

All peoples, clap your hands,
cry to God with shouts of joy!
For the Lord, the Most High, we must fear,
great king over all the earth.

He subdues peoples under us
and nations under our feet.
Our inheritance, our glory, is from him,
given to Jacob out of love.

God goes up with shouts of joy;
the Lord goes up with trumpet blast.
Sing praise for God, sing praise,
sing praise to our king, sing praise.

God is king of all the earth,
sing praise with all your skill.
God is king over the nations;
God reigns on his holy throne.

The princes of the people are assembled
with the people of Abraham's God.
The rulers of the earth belong to God,
to God who reigns over all.

Glory be...

Antiphon
Go, preach the Good News of the kingdom: you received without cost; give without charge.

Reading *2 Corinthians 5:19-20*
God has entrusted to us the news that God and man are reconciled. So we are ambassadors for Christ; it is as though God were appealing through us, and the appeal that we make in Christ's name is: be reconciled with God.

Short Responsory
℟ Tell of the glory of the Lord; announce it among the nations.
℣ Speak of his wonderful deeds to all the peoples.
Glory be…

Benedictus/Magnificat Antiphon
The holy city of Jerusalem had twelve foundation-stones, and on them were the names of the twelve Apostles of the Lamb. The Lamb himself was the light of that city.

Benedictus (if said in the morning) or Magnificat (if said in the evening) - see inside front cover for these prayers

Intercessions
Since we are part of a building that has the Apostles for its foundation, let us pray to the Father for his holy people.

℟ Lord, remember your Church.

Father, when your Son rose from the dead, you showed him first to your Apostles – let us make him known near and far.

℟ Lord, remember your Church.

You sent your Son into the world to proclaim the good news to the poor – grant that we may bring his gospel into the darkness of men's lives.

℟ Lord, remember your Church.

Our Father…

Concluding prayer
Lord God,
you fill your saints with faith and the Holy Spirit
Grant that the gospel which they loved and which they proclaimed with their lives,
may in our day, be faithfully proclaimed by word and deed.
We make our prayer through Christ our Lord.
Amen.

Let us go forward in peace, our eyes upon heaven, the only one goal of our labours.
St Thérèse of Lisieux

Sparks of Light

Wednesday - Even to the shedding of blood

Introduction
O God, come to our aid. Lord, make haste to help us.

Glory be to the Father and to the Son and to the Holy Spirit, as it was in the beginning, is now, and ever shall be, world without end. Amen. (Alleluia)
omit Alleluias during Lent

Hymn
The martyrs living now with Christ
In suffering were tried,
Their anguish overcome by love,
When on his cross they died.

Across the centuries they come,
In constancy unmoved.
Their loving hearts make no complaint;
In silence they are proved.

No man has ever measured love,
Or weighed it in his hand,
But God who knows the inmost heart,
Gives them the promised land.

Praise Father, Son and Spirit blest
Who guide us through the night
In ways that reach beyond the stars
To everlasting light.

Antiphon
When the martyrs of Christ were in torment they fixed their minds on heavenly things, and said: Lord, come to our help.

Psalmody
Psalm 115(116)
I trusted, even when I said:
'I am sorely afflicted,'
and when I said in my alarm:
'No man can be trusted.'

How can I repay the Lord
for his goodness to me?
The cup of salvation I will raise;
I will call on the Lord's name.

My vows to the Lord I will fulfil
before all his people.
O precious in the eyes of the Lord
is the death of his faithful.

Your servant, Lord, your servant am I;
you have loosened my bonds.
A thanksgiving sacrifice I make;
I will call on the Lord's name.

My vows to the Lord I will fulfil
before all his people,
in the courts of the house of the Lord,
in your midst, O Jerusalem.

Antiphon
When the martyrs of Christ were in torment they fixed their minds on heavenly things, and said: Lord, come to our help.

Reading   *2 Corinthians 1:3-5*
Let us give thanks to the God and Father of our Lord Jesus Christ, the merciful Father, the God from whom all help comes: he helps us in all our troubles, so that we are able to help those who have all kinds of troubles, using the same help that we ourselves have received from God. Just as we have a share in Christ's many sufferings, so also through Christ we share in his great help.

Short responsory
℟ The Lord is my strength. I will sing praise to him.
℣ He is my salvation.

Glory be…

Benedictus/Magnificat Antiphon
Blessed are those who are persecuted in the cause of right: theirs is the kingdom of heaven.

Benedictus (if said in the morning)
or Magnificat (if said in the evening) -
see inside front cover for these prayers

Intercessions
Through the martyrs who were slain for God's word, let us give glory to our Saviour, the faithful and true witness.
℟ You redeemed us by your precious blood.

Through the martyrs, who bore witness to your love – set us free to live for you.
℟ You redeemed us by your precious blood.

Through the martyrs, who proclaimed your saving death – give us a deep and constant faith.
℟ You redeemed us by your precious blood.

Through the martyrs, who took up your cross – grant us courage for every trial.
℟ You redeemed us by your precious blood.

Through the martyrs, washed in the blood of the Lamb – give us grace to conquer our weakness.
℟ You redeemed us by your precious blood.

Our Father…

Concluding prayer
Human weakness finds its anchor in you, Lord,
and our faith is built on you as on a rock:
give us a share in the passion and resurrection of Christ through the prayers of your martyrs,
so that we may come to joys that never fail.
We make our prayer through Christ our Lord.
Amen.

Let us go forward in peace, our eyes upon heaven, the only one goal of our labours.
St Thérèse of Lisieux

Sparks of Light

Thursday - In the footsteps of Christ

Introduction
O God, come to our aid. Lord, make haste to help us.

Glory be to the Father and to the Son and to the Holy Spirit, as it was in the beginning, is now, and ever shall be, world without end. Amen. (Alleluia)
omit Alleluias during Lent

Hymn
Let all on earth their voices raise,
Re-echoing Heav'n's triumphant praise
To Him, who gave th' apostles grace
To run on earth their glorious race.

Thou, at Whose word they bore the light
Of Gospel truth o'er heathen night,
To us that heav'nly light impart,
To glad our eyes and cheer our heart.

Thou, at Whose will to them was giv'n
To bind and loose in earth and Heav'n,
Our chains unbind, our sins undo,
And in our hearts Thy grace renew.

Thou, in Whose might they spake the word
Which cured disease and health restored,
To us its healing power prolong,
Support the weak, confirm the strong.

Antiphon
They left their nets and followed their Lord and Redeemer.

Psalmody
Psalm 147

O praise the Lord, Jerusalem!
Zion praise your God!

He has strengthened the bars of your gates
he has blessed the children within you.
He established peace on your borders,
he feeds you with finest wheat.

He sends out his word to the earth
and swiftly runs his command.
He showers down snow white as wool,
he scatters hoar-frost like ashes.

He hurls down hailstones like crumbs.
The waters are frozen at his touch;
he sends forth his word and it melts them:
at the breath of his mouth the waters flow.

He makes his word known to Jacob,
to Israel his laws and decrees.
He has not dealt thus with other nations;
he has not taught them his decrees.

Antiphon
They left their nets and followed their Lord and Redeemer.

Reading *Acts 2:42-45*
They met constantly to hear the Apostles teach, and to share the common life, to break bread, and to pray. A sense of awe was everywhere, and many marvels and signs were brought about through the Apostles. all whose faith had drawn them together held everything in common: they would sell their property and make a general distribution as the need of each required.

Short Responsory
℟ All will know that you are my disciples.
℣ If there is love among you.
Glory be…

Benedictus/Magnificat Antiphon
You did not choose me: I chose you. I appointed you to go on and bear fruit, fruit that shall last.

Benedictus (if said in the morning)
or Magnificat (if said in the evening) - see inside front cover for these prayers

Intercessions
Since we have received from the Apostles our heavenly inheritance, let us thank our Father for all his blessings.
℟ Lord, the Apostles sing your praises.

Praise to you, Lord God, for the gift of Christ's body and blood, handed on by the Apostles, to give us strength and life.
℟ Lord, the Apostles sing your praises.

For the table of the word, served by the Apostles, to bring us light and joy.
℟ Lord, the Apostles sing your praises.

For your holy Church, built on the Apostles, to make us all one body.
℟ Lord, the Apostles sing your praises.

For the washing of baptism and penance, entrusted to the Apostles, to cleanse our hearts from sin.
℟ Lord, the Apostles sing your praises.

Our Father...

Concluding prayer
Almighty God,
you chose the Apostles
and enabled them with grace to preach the good news.
Let their teaching and example so improve our lives
that we may walk faithfully in the footsteps of Christ.
We make our prayer through Christ our Lord.
Amen.

Let us go forward in peace, our eyes upon heaven, the only one goal of our labours.
St Thérèse of Lisieux

Sparks of Light

Friday - A life of virtue

Introduction
O God, come to our aid. Lord, make haste to help us.

Glory be to the Father and to the Son and to the Holy Spirit, as it was in the beginning, is now, and ever shall be, world without end. Amen. (Alleluia)
omit Alleluias during Lent

Hymn
For all the saints, who from their
  labours rest,
Who Thee by faith before the world
  confessed,
Thy Name, O Jesus, be forever blessed.
Alleluia, Alleluia!
(Jublilate, Jubilate!) during Lent

Thou wast their rock, their fortress
  and their might;
Thou, Lord, their captain in the
  well-fought fight;
Thou, in the darkness drear their one
  true Light.
Alleluia, Alleluia!
(Jublilate, Jubilate!) during Lent

O may thy soldiers, faithful, true and bold,
Fight as the saints who nobly fought
  of old,
And win, with them, the victor's crown
  of gold.
Alleluia, Alleluia!
(Jublilate, Jubilate!) during Lent

O blest communion! fellowship divine!
We fight as they did, 'neath the holy sign;
And all are one in thee, for all are thine.
Alleluia, Alleluia!
(Jublilate, Jubilate!) during Lent

Antiphon
My soul clings to you; your right hand holds me fast.

Psalmody
Psalm 62 (63)
O God, you are my God, for you I long;
for you my soul is thirsting.
My body pines for you
like a dry, weary land without water.
So I gaze on you in the sanctuary
to see your strength and your glory.

For your love is better than life,
my lips will speak your praise.
So I will bless you all my life,
in your name I will lift up my hands.
My soul shall be filled as with a banquet,
my mouth shall praise you with joy.

On my bed I remember you.
On you I muse through the night
for your have been my help;
in the shadow of your wings I rejoice.
My soul clings to you;
your right hand holds me fast.

Antiphon
My soul clings to you; your right hand holds me fast.

Reading *Romans 12:1-2*
I implore you by God's mercy to offer your very selves to him: a living sacrifice, dedicated and fit for his acceptance, the worship offered by mind and heart. Adapt yourselves no longer to the pattern of this present world, but let your minds be remade and your whole nature thus

transformed. Then you will be able to discern the will of God, and to know what is good, acceptable and perfect.

Short Responsory
℟ The just shall rejoice in the sight of God.
℣ They shall be filled with gladness.
Glory be…

Benedictus/Magnificat Antiphon
The Lord is all that I have; the Lord is good to the soul that seeks him.

Benedictus (if said in the morning) or Magnificat (if said in the evening) - see inside front cover for these prayers

Intercessions
Let us praise Christ, the holy God, and ask that we may serve him in justice and holiness all the days of our life.

℟ Lord, you alone are holy.

You were tempted in every way that we are, but you did not sin – Lord Jesus, have mercy on us.

℟ Lord, you alone are holy.

You have called us to grow in love until there is no longer any fear – Lord Jesus, make us holy.

℟ Lord, you alone are holy.

In a world of human need it was your will to serve and not to be served – let us become like you, Lord Jesus, in the humble service of others.

Our Father…

Concluding prayer
Almighty, ever-living God,
who in the lives of the saints
continually give us proofs of your love:
lead us to the faithful imitation of Christ,
by the help of their prayer and the
  spur of their example.
We make our prayer through Christ our
  Lord.
Amen.

Let us go forward in peace, our eyes upon heaven, the only one goal of our labours.
St Thérèse of Lisieux

Sparks of Light

Saturday - Mary, Shelter of the Word

Introduction
O God, come to our aid. Lord, make haste to help us.

Glory be to the Father and to the Son and to the Holy Spirit, as it was in the beginning, is now, and ever shall be, world without end. Amen. (Alleluia)
omit Alleluias during Lent

Hymn
Mary, crowned with living light,
Temple of the Lord,
Place of peace and holiness,
Shelter of the Word.

Mystery of sinless life
In our fallen race,
Free from shadow you reflect
Plenitude of grace.

Virgin-mother of our God,
Lift us when we fall,
Who were named upon the Cross
Mother of us all.

Father, Son and Holy Ghost,
Heaven sings your praise,
Mary magnifies your name
through eternal days.

Antiphon
The mother of Jesus said: Do whatever he tells you.

Psalmody   *Canticle 21 (Ephesians 1:3-10)*
Blest be the God and Father
of our Lord Jesus Christ,
who has blessed us in Christ
with every spiritual blessing
  in the heavenly places.

He chose us in him
before the foundation of the world,
that we should be holy
and blameless before him.

He destined us in love
to be his sons through Jesus Christ,
according to the purpose of his will,
to the praise of his glorious grace
which he freely bestowed on us in the
  Beloved.

In him we have redemption through
  his blood,
the forgiveness of our trespasses,
according to the riches of his grace
which he lavished upon us.

He has made known to us
in all wisdom and insight
the mystery of his will,
according to his purpose
that he set forth in Christ.

His purpose he set forth in Christ
as a plan for the fullness of time,
to unite all things in him,
things in heaven and things on earth.

Antiphon
The mother of Jesus said: Do whatever he tells you.

Reading   *Galatians 4:4-5*
When the appointed time came, God sent his Son, born of a woman, born a subject of the Law, to redeem the subjects of the Law and to enable us to be adopted as sons.

Short responsory
℟ The Lord chose her. He chose her before she was born.
℣ He made her live in his own dwelling place.
Glory be…

Benedictus/Magnificat Antiphon
Blessed are you, Mary, because you believed that all those things which were said to you by the Lord will be fulfilled.

Benedictus (if said in the morning)
or Magnificat (if said in the evening) - see inside front cover for these prayers

Intercessions
Let us praise God the Father who chose Mary as the mother of his Son and wanted all generations to call her blessed. With confidence we pray:

℟ May the Virgin Mary intercede for us.

Father, you did great things for the Virgin Mary and brought her, body and soul, to the glory of heaven – fill the hearts of your children with the hope of Christ's glory.

℟ May the Virgin Mary intercede for us.

Through the prayers of Mary, our mother, heal the sick, comfort the sorrowful, pradon sinners – grant peace and salvation to all

℟ May the Virgin Mary intercede for us.

You favoured Mary with the fullness of grace – bestow on all your overflowing blessings.

℟ May the Virgin Mary intercede for us.

Our Father…

Concluding prayer
Lord our God,
you bestowed the Holy Spirit on your
  Apostles while they were at prayer with
  Mary the Mother of Jesus:
grant that by her prayer
we may give you faithful service
and spread abroad the glory of your
  name by word and example.
We make our prayer through Christ our
  Lord.
Amen.

Let us go forward in peace, our eyes upon heaven, the only one goal of our labours.
St Thérèse of Lisieux

Sparks of Light

Supplementary resources

- Quotes on holiness and sanctity
- The Daily Decalogue of Blessed Pope John XXIII
- Your Roadmap for Sainthood
- The Saints and You
- Filmography & Bibiliography

Quotes on holiness and sanctity

God invites us all to sainthood
All of us can attain to Christian virtue and holiness, no matter in what condition of life we live and no matter what our life work may be.
St Francis de Sales (1567-1622)

God's invitation to become saints is for all, not just a few. Sanctity therefore must be accessible to all. In what does it consist? In a lot of activity? No. In doing extraordinary things? No, this could not be for everybody and at all times. Therefore, sanctity consists in doing good, and in doing this good in whatever condition and place God has placed us. Nothing more, nothing outside of this.
Blessed Louis Tezza (1841-1923)

Our Lord has created persons for all states in life, and in all of them we see people who achieved sanctity by fulfilling their obligations well.
St Anthony Mary Claret (1807-1870)

What God wants most of all for each one of you is that you should become holy. He loves you much more than you could ever begin to imagine, and he wants the very best for you. And by far the best thing for you is to grow in holiness.
Pope Benedict XVI in 2010

The example of the saints is proposed to every one, so that the great actions shown us may encourage us to undertake smaller things.
Venerable Louis de Granada (1505-1588)

In small steps and little ways
Certainly our goal is both lofty and difficult to attain. But please do not forget that people are not born holy. Holiness is forged through a constant interplay of God's grace and the correspondence of man. As one of the early Christian writers says, referring to union with God, 'Everything that grows begins small. It is by constant and progressive feeding that it gradually grows big'. So I say to you, if you want to become a thorough-going Christian – and I know you are willing, even though you often find it difficult to conquer yourself or to keep climbing upwards with this poor body of ours – then you will have to be very attentive to the minutest of details, for the holiness that Our Lord demands of you is to be achieved by carrying out with love of God your work and your daily duties, and these will almost always consist of small realities.
St Josemaría Escrivá (1902-1975)

Here, we make sanctity consist in always being cheerful.
St Dominic Savio (1842-1857)

Sparks of Light

I have always wanted to become a saint. Unfortunately when I have compared myself with the saints, I have always found that there is the same difference between the saints and me as there is between a mountain whose summit is lost in the clouds and a humble grain of sand trodden underfoot by passers-by. Instead of being discouraged, I told myself: God would not make me wish for something impossible and so, in spite of my littleness, I can aim at being a saint. It is impossible for me to grow bigger, so I put up with myself as I am, with all my countless faults. But I will look for some means of going to heaven by a little way which is very short and very straight, a little way that is quite new.

St Thérèse of Lisieux (1873-1897)

You learn to speak by speaking, to study by studying, to run by running, to work by working, and just so, you learn to love by loving. All those who think to learn in any other way deceive themselves.

St Francis de Sales (1567-1622)

Trials and tribulations
The more a person loves God, the more reason he has to hope in Him. This hope produces in the Saints an unutterable peace, which they preserve even in adversity, because as they love God, and know how beautiful He is to those who love Him, they place all their confidence and find all their repose in Him alone.

St Alphonsus Liguori (1696-1787)

If God gives you an abundant harvest of trials, it is a sign of great holiness which He desires you to attain. Do you want to become a great saint? Ask God to send you many sufferings. The flame of Divine Love never rises higher than when fed with the wood of the Cross, which the infinite charity of the Saviour used to finish His sacrifice. All the pleasures of the world are nothing compared with the sweetness found in the gall and vinegar offered to Jesus Christ. That is, hard and painful things endured for Jesus Christ and with Jesus Christ.

St Ignatius of Loyola (1491-1556)

There is no surer way to know that one is a saint than to see him lead a holy life and yet suffer desolation, trials and tribulations.

St Aloysius Gonzaga (1568-1591)

God does not forsake you. It is because he wishes to increase your glory that oftentimes he permits you to fall sick. Keep up your courage so that you may also hear him say: 'Do you think I have dealt with you otherwise than that you may be shown to be just?'

St John Chrysostom (344-407)

Following the Will of God
Lord, those are your best servants who wish to shape their life on Your answers rather than to shape Your answers on their wishes.
St Augustine of Hippo (354-430)

Do not be conformed to this world, but be transformed by the renewing of your minds, so that you may discern what is the will of God - what is good and acceptable and perfect.
Romans 12:2

We must have a real living determination to reach holiness. I will be a saint means I will despoil myself of all that is not God; I will strip my heart of all created things; I will live in poverty and detachment; I will renounce my will, my inclinations, my whims and fancies, and make myself a willing slave to the will of God.
Blessed Mother Teresa (1910-1997)

O my Jesus and my Love, take all that I have and all that I am and possess me to the full extent of Thy good pleasure, since all I have is Thine without reserve. Transform me entirely into Thyself, so that I may no longer be able to separate myself from Thee for a single moment, and that I may no longer act but by the impulse of Thy pure love.
St Margaret Mary Alacoque (1647-1690)

By God's Grace
Holiness is a disposition of the heart that makes us humble and little in the arms of God, aware of our weakness, and confident - in the most audacious way - in His Fatherly goodness.
St Thérèse of Lisieux (1873-1897)

Nothing whatever pertaining to godliness and real holiness can be accomplished without grace.
St Augustine of Hippo (354-430)

God creates out of nothing. Wonderful you say. Yes, to be sure, but he does what is still more wonderful: he makes saints out of sinners
Søren Kierkegaard (1813-1855)

Pursue with invincible courage the end to which you have been called; God has furnished such help and means to aid you in attaining it.
St Ignatius of Loyola (1491-1556)

God's ways are incomprehensible. He uses very sharp files, which penetrate the heart and remove the rust. His files are all spiritual.
St Paul of the Cross (1694-1775)

Sparks of Light

Living for others
Give something, however small, to the one in need. For it is not small to one who has nothing. Neither is it small to God, if we have given what we could.

St Gregory Nazianzen (c.329-389)

On the question of relating to our fellowman – our neighbour's spiritual need transcends every commandment. Everything else we do is a means to an end. But love is an end already, since God is love.

St Teresia Benedicta of the Cross (Edith Stein), (1891-1942)

The life of the saints is the norm of living for others.

St Ambrose of Milan (339-397)

However!
Do not give yourself entirely to activity and do not engage in active works all the time. Keep something of your heart and of your time for meditation.

St Bernard of Clairvaux (1090-1153)

The Beatitudes (Matthew 5:1-12)
Now when he saw the crowds, he went up on a mountainside and sat down. His disciples came to Him, and He began to teach them, saying:

Blessed are the poor in spirit, for theirs is the kingdom of heaven.

Blessed are those who mourn, for they will be comforted.

Blessed are the meek, for they will inherit the earth.

Blessed are those who hunger and thirst after righteousness, for they will be filled.

Blessed are the merciful, for they shall be shown mercy.

Blessed are the pure in heart, for they will see God.

Blessed are the peacemakers, for they will be called the sons of God.

Blessed are those who are persecuted because of righteousness, for theirs is the kingdom of heaven.

Blessed are you when people insult you, persecute you and falsely say all kinds of evil against you because of me.

Rejoice and be glad, because great is your reward in heaven, for in the same way they persecuted the prophets who were before you.

A final thought
If you are what you should be, you will set the whole world ablaze!

St Catherine of Siena (1347-1380)

The Daily Decalogue of Blessed Pope John XXIII

1. **Only for today**, I will seek to live the livelong day positively without wishing to solve the problems of my life all at once.

2. **Only for today**, I will take the greatest care of my appearance: I will dress modestly; I will not raise my voice; I will be courteous in my behaviour; I will not criticise anyone; I will not claim to improve or to discipline anyone except myself.

3. **Only for today**, I will be happy in the certainty that I was created to be happy, not only in the other world but also in this one.

4. **Only for today**, I will adapt to circumstances, without requiring all circumstances to be adapted to my own wishes.

5. **Only for today**, I will devote 10 minutes of my time to some good reading, remembering that just as food is necessary to the life of the body, so good reading is necessary to the life of the soul.

6. **Only for today**, I will do one good deed and not tell anyone about it.

7. **Only for today**, I will do at least one thing I do not like doing; and if my feelings are hurt, I will make sure that no one notices.

8. **Only for today**, I will make a plan for myself: I may not follow it to the letter, but I will make it. And I will be on guard against two evils: hastiness and indecision.

9. **Only for today**, I will firmly believe, despite appearances, that the good Providence of God cares for me as no one else who exists in this world.

10. **Only for today**, I will have no fears. In particular, I will not be afraid to enjoy what is beautiful and to believe in goodness. Indeed, for 12 hours I can certainly do what might cause me consternation were I to believe I had to do it all my life.

Sparks of Light

Your Roadmap for Sainthood!
complete this form when you have time

'In short there are three things that last: faith, hope and love' (1 Corinthians 13:13). These three virtues are the bedrock of a Christian life; they give life to all that is good in us and show the presence and action of the Holy Spirit in our lives. The journey to holiness is a lifelong one where the practice of virtue and the following of the gospel require perseverance and deliberate actions. Use the space below to reflect on your life so far and to look ahead to the months and years yet to come.

How has your life been built on and marked by Faith?
Faith is the theological virtue by which we believe in God and believe all that he has said and revealed to us, and that Holy Church proposes for our belief, because he is truth itself (CCC, 1814).

What part has Hope played in the way that you see the world?
Hope is the theological virtue by which we desire the kingdom of heaven and eternal life as our happiness, placing our trust in Christ's promises and relying not on our own strength, but on the help of the grace of the Holy Spirit (CCC, 1817).

Sparks of Light

When in your life have you shown the virtue of Charity?
Charity is the theological virtue by which we love God above all things for his own sake, and our neighbour as ourselves for the love of God (CCC, 1822).

In what ways do you feel you are being invited to grow?

The Saints and You

Small groups across the world have found it very helpful to ask for the intercession of a particular saint. They have adoped the name of their favourite saint and refer to themselves by his or her name (e.g. St Martin de Porres Small Community).

- Perhaps you would consider adopting a saint as patron for your group.

Several parishes hold special events on the anniversary of their parish saint. A large fair, an open day, a parish meal, a whole parish Mass are all great ways of bringing the parish together while paying respect to its patron.

- Perhaps you would consider organising a special event on your parish feast day.

Individuals and families find it useful to adopt a patron. This may be a favourite saint or it may be one that the Church has given patronage to your profession or place. Indeed you may already have a saint, one you chose at confirmation.

- Perhaps you would look to research and celebrate the life of your Confirmation saint or email us who your favourite saint is and why.

Sparks of Light

Filmography

films about the saints are wonderful ways to explore their lives and their motivation

Love is a Choice: The Life of St. Gianna Beretta Molla (Ignatius) [52mins - NTSC only]

Sanctity Within Reach: Pier Giorgio Frassati (EWTN) [90mins - 3 part mini-series]

Bakhita: From Slave to Saint (Ignatius) [190mins - NTSC only]

Catholic Saints of England (Marys Dowry Productions) [35mins - PAL]
Preview: http://www.youtube.com/watch?v=p5DBBx2dAz4
Order: http://www.marysdowryproductions.org

Saints - helping us today (Catholic Faith Exploration, CaFE - PAL/NTSC)
A six session DVD course that would be an excellent follow-up to *Sparks of Light*
Order: http://www.ctshop.org/acatalog/Saints.html#a177

Vision: From the life of Hildegard of Bingen (Zeitgeist Films) [110mins - NTSC only]

Watch out for *Cristiada* (post-production as of January 2012) which looks at the Mexican Cristero war in the 1920s.

In Search of St John Southworth (2011) Diocese of Westminster
Preview: http://vimeo.com/32845828

Also on sacrifice *Of Gods and Men* (Artificial Eye) [122mins - PAL/NTSC]

And pilgrimage and holiness *The Way* (Icon Home) [123mins - PAL/NTSC]

NOTE: NTSC is the video format used in the US and Japan and will not work on most UK DVD players. PAL is the format used in Europe and Australia except France which uses SECAM

Sparks of Light

Bibliography

naturally this bibliography cannot be considered exhaustive but serves as a useful starting point

On Holiness
William O'Malley (2008) *Holiness (Catholic Spirituality for Adults)*, Orbis

Benedict XVI (2011) *Holiness is Always in Season*, Ignatius Press

R. Richard Thomas (2002) *The Ordinary Path to Holiness*, St Paul's Publishing

Eric Sammons (March 2012) *Holiness for Everyone: The Practical Spirituality of St Josemaría Escrivá*, Our Sunday Visitor

Richard Rohr (2011) *Breathing Under Water: Spirituality and the Twelve Steps*, St Anthony Messenger Press

St John of the Cross (2011) *Sayings of Light and Love*, WRCDT

Dei Verbum (especially chapter VI) – http://tinyurl.com/deiverbum

Lumen Gentium (especially chapters II and V) – http://tinyurl.com/onthechurch

On the Saints
Lisa Hendey (2011) *A Book of Saints for Catholic Moms: 52 Companions for Your Heart, Mind, Body, and Soul*, Ava Maria Press

Luciana Frassati (1990) *A Man of the Beatitudes: Pier Giorgio Frassati*, ignatius Press

Pietro Molla & Elio Guerriero (2004) *Saint Gianna Molla*, Ignatius Press

Spe Salvi (especially sections 3 and 5) – http://tinyurl.com/savedinhope

For more on the Year of Faith (October 2012 to November 2013)
Benedict XVI (2011) *Porta Fidei* – http://tinyurl.com/dooroffaith

Sparks of Light

Notes